# Contemporary Wedding Services

## John Killinger

ABINGDON PRESS

Nashville

CONTEMPORARY WEDDING SERVICES

*Copyright © 1986 by Abingdon Press*

*This book is printed on acid-free paper.*

**Library of Congress Cataloging-in-Publication Data**

**Killinger, John.**
  **Contemporary wedding services.**

  1. Marriage service. I. Title.
  BV199.M3K55    1986    265′.5    86-8083
  ISBN 0-687-09522-0 (alk. paper)

All Scripture quotations, unless otherwise marked, are from the King James Version of the Bible.

All Scripture quotations marked NEB are from The New English Bible. Copyright © the Delegates of the Oxford University Press and the Syndics of the Cambridge University Press 1961, 1970. Reprinted by permission.

MANUFACTURED IN THE UNITED STATES OF AMERICA

# CONTENTS

# INTRODUCTION

A wedding is undeniably one of the most sacred moments in life. It is sacred for the bride and groom. It is sacred for their attendants and families. And it is sacred for most of the persons in the congregation, all of whom are touched by the mystery of the service and what it means to the future of those taking vows.

It is important, therefore, that the service be as fitting as possible for each couple. Couples differ greatly in mood, style, and temperament. The service that would be appropriate for one couple might be entirely wrong for another.

Ministers who counsel couples before their weddings are often aware of this, yet they lack a variety of services from which to choose. They resort, out of necessity, to the traditional service of their particular communion, breathing a prayer of petition to God to make everything all right despite the unsuitability of the liturgy.

The services in this book are prepared to serve the need of the pastor in today's world by providing a variety of fresh, deeply Christian liturgies that can be used with confidence to join couples for whom older, traditional services seem somehow inadequate or inexpressive. They are not intended to replace services already in use—only to supplement them.

The services are designed to permit a maximum of flexibility in their use. Parts of one service may be combined with parts of another or of several services to produce one deemed most suitable for a particular couple. Or parts may be used to replace certain portions of older, more familiar services to bring to them a fresh note, like a new accent piece in a room filled with old furniture.

Several of the services are designed to be used with couples of any age. But there is also one for an older couple with children and one for an elderly couple. And there are services for use at Christmas and Easter time, reflecting the influence of these special seasons of the Christian year.

The emphasis throughout is on the wedding as a holy act, as something done before God and, therefore, as a worship experience. Worship settings are not provided, but can easily be imagined.

In many churches the minister, groom, and best man will appear; the wedding march will bring the attendants and bride to the front of the sanctuary to join them; and a hymn will be sung, followed by scriptures and prayers, and even a meditation on marriage, before the service from this book is commenced. After the joining of the couple as husband and wife, there may be a hymn and shared communion before the final prayer and recessional.

In the church where I am the minister, each service is neatly printed and bound in an attractive wedding folder. The minister reads the service from this copy and afterward presents it to the bride and groom.

If an order of service is desired for the congregation, it may be easily compiled in correlation to the various sections of the service designated in this book.

Some ministers will wish to provide copies of *Contemporary Wedding Services* to prospective brides and grooms, in order that they may consider the various services before selecting one. The bride and groom may also be apprised of the possibility of substituting certain sections in one service for those in another.

I have found that this procedure makes the couple much more conscious of the language of the chosen service and actually heightens their appreciation of the spiritual nature of the step they are taking. The discussion of the wording of a particular passage—say, of the vows or a prayer—will often lead to a profitable discussion of the individuals' faith and religious commitment or of their understanding of marriage, and thus will become an aid to counseling.

Any minister with an aptitude for composing liturgies is encouraged to develop his or her own file of expressive and useful wedding services. These may, in turn, be added to the several options in this book and presented to the couple for their consideration.

*Contemporary Wedding Services,* in other words, is not meant to become the minister's exclusive source of new wedding material. It is intended as a supplement and an encouragement—an encouragement to be open and sensitive to the needs and life-style of each couple approaching marriage, and to attempt to fit to those needs and that life-style a beautifully adapted wedding service.

JOHN KILLINGER

# I.

---

# A SERVICE FOR
# GENERAL USE,
# I

## THE PROLOGUE

People were not made to live alone. We know ourselves, experience ourselves, enjoy ourselves in relation to other human beings. Other persons sharpen our perceptions, shape our ideas, mold our personalities, engage our wits, challenge our ingenuities, enlarge our sympathies. For this reason there are tribes, cities, nations, institutions. For this reason, too, there is marriage. In fact, of all the relationships that mold, challenge, and sensitize, there is none like marriage—none so intimate; none so threatening; none so filled with potential for helping and hurting, blessing and cursing, shaping and destroying.

For this reason, marriage should never be entered into lightly, without a deep sense of reverence and commitment. In the biblical sense, two persons who marry become one flesh, one corporate person, for better or worse the rest of their lives. Their souls may sometimes be at odds, pulling and straining against one another, but the conflict still occurs within a single flesh. This is why quarreling and disagreement within the marriage body are so painful—it is like quarreling with oneself, with another aspect of one's own life. It is also why there is no joy quite like the joy of a married couple who have grown adjusted to each other, for they have deepened each other's capacity to experience everything until they feel the delights of life doubly, triply, and even more.

We are gathered here this evening to witness the official moment of marriage between _____ and _____ and to celebrate their union in a time of fellowship.

It is a family time, for what they do here will long affect both families being united. It is also a religious time, because marriage, since biblical times, has had its roots in faith and tradition. We read in the scriptures that Jesus attended a wedding at Cana of Galilee, where he turned water into wine. And he often used the symbolism of wedded joy to describe the ecstasy of his followers whenever he is present with them. Therefore what we do here is done not only before the respective families, but also before God himself, whose witness to these moments will seal them long after the rest of us have passed from earthly scenes.

## THE GIVING OF THE BRIDE

Who blesses _____ as she marries _____?

Let us have a prayer for the families of _____ and _____, who have given their blessings to this union:

O God of all marriages, whose will is that we be one family in our Lord Jesus Christ, we lift up before you the families of _____ and _____, and ask your special favor upon them. Grant them a sense of the wonderful opportunity that is theirs for growth and understanding through their new relationships with each other. Make them loving and generous to each other in all their dealings. Teach the parents to give up their children in order to find them again in new and exciting ways. Let your peace and fullness abide on them this day and in all time to come. Through Jesus Christ our Lord. **Amen.**

## THE EXCHANGE OF RINGS AND VOWS

_____ and _____, in the vows which you are about to make, if you are sincere and faithful in your attempts to honor them, if you love each other truly enough to try to be open to growth and change, each for the other, and if you are careful in your lives to remember God daily and submit yourselves to him and his kingdom, then God will bless your union and you will begin a pilgrimage together that will enrich you as nothing else in life is able to do.

Do you have the rings you intend to give to each other? Let us have a prayer of blessing for them:

Lord, these lovely rings are seamless, like the round of the years in your sight, like the love that _____ and _____ feel for each other at this time. May they become golden shields, guarding their care for each other, that it may deepen and broaden through the years by reminding them of their commitment to each other and to you. **Amen.**

_____, will you place your ring on _____'s finger, and then continue to hold her hand as you repeat your wedding promise:

**With this ring I wed you, and bring to you all that I am and all that I have, that we two may become one for better, for worse, in good health and bad, in sunshine and shadow for the remainder of our lives. I hope always to love you. I promise always, as far as I am able, to put your happiness above my own and to be faithful to the spirit of this moment.**

_____, will you place your ring on _____'s finger, and then continue to hold her hand as you repeat the same promise after me:

**With this ring I wed you, and bring to you all that I am and all that I have, that we two may become one for better, for worse, in good health and bad, in sunshine and shadow for the remainder of our**

**lives. I hope always to love you. I promise always, as far as I am able, to put your happiness above my own and to be faithful to the spirit of this moment.**

## THE PRONOUNCEMENT

_____ and _____, because you have given your promise to love and honor each other for the rest of your lives, I now name you husband and wife. If you wish, you may seal the occasion with an embrace and a kiss.

## THE BLESSING

Now let us pray:

Our Father, life is full of your grace and beauty, and we are grateful for the eyes to behold this. Yet it is also often a struggle, a pilgrimage in which we learn things we wish we had known in the beginning. We pray for _____ and _____ as they begin their journey. Teach them how to share so intimately all their thoughts, hopes, and fears that each will take courage from the other, and learn to deal more confidently with himself or herself and with life. Let them learn quickly how to express love within the marriage relationship, that in expressing it they may also discover how to love better. Grant that they may be accepting and forgiving of each other's faults and shortcomings, that each may more readily deal with his or her inner problems in such a supportive atmosphere. Teach them patience and kindness, and excitement in each other's differences, that they may see themselves complemented and enriched, each in the other, instead of threatened or challenged by diversity. If it is your will to bless them with children, grant them strength, wisdom, and tolerance to be helpful, caring parents. Give them a sense of humor about themselves and their relationship, that they may keep their smaller differences and misunderstandings in true perspective.

Bless their larger families with the grace to be good relations, who prove supportive in times of need and loving and encouraging at all other times as well. And, above all and in all, grant them a steady awareness of your loving presence, that they may live with the assurance of the meaning of their relationship and existence, knowing that what we have now sealed here is guaranteed by the name that is above every name, even Jesus Christ our Lord, who has taught us to pray, saying:

**Our Father which art in heaven, Hallowed be thy name. Thy kingdom come. Thy will be done in earth, as it is in heaven. Give us this day our daily bread. And forgive us our debts, as we forgive our debtors. And lead us not into temptation, but deliver us from evil: For thine is the kingdom, and the power, and the glory for ever. Amen.**

# II.

---

# A SERVICE FOR
# GENERAL USE,
# II

## THE PROLOGUE

The world is changing every day; institutions rise and institutions fall. But one thing does not change. The institution of marriage remains the foundation of all civilization, and one of the greatest occasions for joy and excitement we shall ever know.

It was no accident that Jesus Christ repeatedly spoke of his kingdom in the metaphor of marriage or the marriage feast. The splendor of an ancient wedding—with guests coming from far and wide and staying for many days; with festive meals and singing and dancing; with gifts and speeches; with parades, canopies, and sacred processions; with prayers, embraces, and the saying of vows—became the image of what it means to be joined in union with God, to be part of the church, which is the bride of Christ, and to be mystically bound forever in a communion of holiness, transcendent in time and space and thought.

As we engage today in the wedding of _____ and _____, we perpetuate that image, imbuing it with freshness and power; and, in the same manner, the reality of the kingdom, won by Christ in his sorrowful death and wondrous resurrection, validates what we do with a holy validation, timely in the hour and eternal in the heavens.

## THE GIVING OF THE BRIDE

_____ and _____ have confessed their love to each other in moments both private and tender, and now they appear before us in a place sanctified by prayer and praise to confess it publicly, and to be joined by mutual pledge in a lifelong compact of marriage. For as long as anyone can remember, it has been traditional at such moments for the parents of those being united to bestow upon them their sincerest blessings of good will.

Who blesses _____ as she marries _____?

Let us pray for the families of _____ and _____, who have given their blessing to this union:

O God, who in infinite wisdom has provided families as the protecting and nurturing units of our natural existence, we thank you for the families of _____ and _____ and for the strength, character, and joy with which they have outfitted them through the years. Now, as they have given their blessing to this marriage and so surrendered part of their own bodies and spirits to its beginning, we ask for them a sense of glad fulfillment that surpasses any feelings of loss or bereavement. Let them behold in this union a symbol of our greater communion with you, and so profit by becoming part of one another, a greater family than they have known.

Teach the parents to be wise mentors of married children, supporting with tact, guiding with generosity, and being present in love. Remove all jealousy, distrust, and fear, and give to each a sense of your Holy Spirit, operating in all of us to bring us unto a happy consummation in Christ Jesus, to whom be glory forever and ever. **Amen.**

## THE EXCHANGE OF RINGS AND VOWS

_____ and _____, we come now to the sacred moment when you make your vows of love and faithfulness to each other. Vows and oaths are never to be taken lightly, especially when they are made before God in the company of other believers. They are like anchors that hold us steady in the storms and gales of life: If you are sincere in the words you say to each other, and if you will remember them as long as you live, they will prove important guides in seasons of distress and indecision. Moreover, the

23

God who hears your vows will be present to aid you in keeping them whenever you repeat them in awareness of God's spirit.

May I have the rings you intend to give each other, that we may invoke a divine blessing upon them?

O God, who mediates yourself to us in earthly symbols, that we may touch and taste and handle that which otherwise would remain remote and hidden, we offer for your blessing these rings that _____ and _____ will wear as memories of this moment. Anoint them with the power to recall for _____ and _____ their vows of loving and caring, that in all the hard or barren places of life, when each is tempted to feel forlorn or to undertake a separate journey, they may find healing where there was woundedness and affection where estrangement. Through him who was wounded for our transgressions and bruised for our iniquities. **Amen.**

_____, as you look into _____'s face and place your ring on her finger, will you please repeat after me the words of your promise to her:

**I, _____, take you, _____, to be my life's companion. I choose to share with you my hearth and home, my work and play, and my burdens and joys. I promise you my love, my respect, and my**

devotion as we travel life's way. And I ask God's help in keeping this vow I have made to you.

_____, as you look into _____'s face and place your ring on his finger, will you please repeat after me the words of your promise to him:

I, _____, take you, _____, to be my life's companion. I choose to share with you my hearth and home, my work and play, and my burdens and joys. I promise you my love, my respect, and my devotion as we travel life's way. And I ask God's help in keeping this vow I have made to you.

## THE PRONOUNCEMENT

_____ and _____, your love for each other has brought you together, and in the sanctuaries of your hearts has already made you one. Now, in the presence of God and this gathering, I bless your marriage and pronounce you husband and wife. May your lives become ever more richly entwined and may God sanctify your union unto all future generations in the name of the Father, Son, and Holy Ghost. If you wish, you may kiss and embrace each other before we pray.

## THE BLESSING

Let us pray:
O God, who presides over hearth and home as the guarantor of all that is good and holy, we invoke

your special care upon the journey of _____ and _____ from this day forward in their lives. Give them, we ask, the grace of patience and endurance, that they may find strength and hope in their partnership and discover those deeper resources of the marriage relationship that are one of its truest reasons for being. If it is your will to bless their union with children, give them the love and wisdom to be good parents, providing both the physical and emotional environment for a healthy, happy family. Help them to take their relationship seriously, always being faithful to the vows they have made today, and yet to laugh at themselves, seeing their mistakes and shortcomings from the perspective of Christian security.

Grant that they may learn to value those things that are of true and lasting value, and never to form their lives or attitudes around things that perish with the age. Let a sense of your eternal presence be and abide in their home from this day forth, and let them draw from that presence the influence that will shape them and their relationship not only for life but also for life beyond death. And so order it that this may be for all of us a time for remembering the vows we have made and renewing our commitments to you, in the name of him who taught us to pray, saying:

**Our Father which art in heaven, Hallowed be thy name. Thy kingdom come. Thy will be done in**

earth, as it is in heaven. Give us this day our daily bread. And forgive us our debts, as we forgive our debtors. And lead us not into temptation, but deliver us from evil: For thine is the kingdom, and the power, and the glory for ever. Amen.

# III.

---

# A SERVICE FOR

# GENERAL USE,

# III

## THE PROLOGUE

*How beautiful you are, my dearest,*
*O how beautiful,*
*your eyes are like doves!*

*How beautiful you are, O my love,*
*and how pleasant!*
(Song of Songs 1:15 NEB)

The words are from the poet of the Song of Songs. They are the speeches of a bridegroom and a bride to each other on the eve of their wedding. They express the delight a man and woman find in each other and the joy they feel as they come before the priest to be made husband and wife in the eyes of God. Thus is the ceremony of Christian marriage embedded in the age-old practices of religion. From time immemorial people have gathered to celebrate the courtship and union of two persons who love each other, and we who assemble here today stand in the tradition of that celebration. We are gathered in a place sanctified by the holiest rites of our faith to solemnize the vows of marriage for _____ and _____, who confess their belief in God and their commitment to following the ways taught by our Lord Jesus Christ.

No celebration of a ritual moment in the church is ever for the participants alone. It is for all of us a time of holiness, when our own vows are renewed and our sensibilities heightened. Therefore, we participate not as onlookers but as actors, silently and spiritually enacting our own parts before God.

Our focus, of course, is on _____ and _____ and on their families, who are being brought together in important new ways through this ceremony. They all stand on the threshold of many experiences that will broaden and deepen their sympathies as human beings. Let us ask, therefore, who gives a blessing upon _____ as she comes to be married to _____. By tradition it is assumed that the groom's family members bestow their blessing upon him as he stands before us to represent them in the union. Let us pray for these families being united:

O God of all marriages, whose will is that we be one family in our Lord Jesus Christ, we lift up before you the families of _____ and _____ and ask your favor upon them. Grant them a sense of the opportunity that is theirs for growth through their new relationships. Make them loving and generous to one another in all their dealings. Teach them to give up their children in order to find them again in new and wonderful ways. Let your peace and fullness abide on them this day and in all time to come. Through Jesus Christ our Lord. **Amen.**

## THE EXCHANGE OF RINGS AND VOWS

Now _____ and _____, we come to the solemn moment of your making vows of marriage to each other. Vows are an ancient part of the marriage ceremony. The earliest vows of which we read in the Bible were between God and his people; they were part of the covenant relationship. Perhaps this is why Jesus spoke of the church as the bride of Christ—because the church was the fulfillment of that relationship. And it is why the vows in any marriage contract are so important, because they are set in the context of what God has done for his people.

If you are true to the spirit of the vows which you are about to make, and regard them with the kind of holiness they truly deserve, they will become a blessing to you all of your lives. They will be the anchors that steady you in times of self-doubt. They will be the stars that guide you in the dark night of moral confusion. They will be the iron tracks that carry you safely on your way through the wilderness of human experience.

Are you willing to proceed to the taking of vows? Then let us pray:

Our wills are ours, O God, in order to make them yours. We stand in your presence now with an awareness of the seriousness of what we are about to do. Hear our words and bind them upon our hearts, that we may serve you in the observance of them for all time to come. Through him who was obedient even unto death, Christ Jesus, our Lord. **Amen.**

_____, will you please place your ring upon _____'s finger, and, continuing to hold her hand, repeat the following words after me:

**I, _____, receive you, _____, as my dearly beloved wife. I promise to care for you as long as we both shall live and to place your well-being above my own. I shall love you, guard you, and provide for you with all my strength. I shall pray for our lives to become so entwined that neither knows the one apart from the other, and I declare myself open for growth and change in any manner that will profit the two of us as we pursue our journey under God.**

_____, will you please place your ring upon _____'s finger, and, continuing to hold his hand, repeat the following words after me:

I, _____, receive you, _____, as my dearly beloved husband. I promise to care for you as long as we both shall live and to place your well-being above my own. I shall love you, honor you, and seek to help you with all of my strength. I, too, shall pray for our lives to become so entwined that neither knows the one apart from the other, and I, too, declare myself open for growth and change in any manner that will profit the two of us on our journey under God.

## THE PRONOUNCEMENT

_____ and _____, because your families have given their blessings to your union, and because you have spoken your vows truly to each other, I declare upon my authority as an ordained minister of the church of Jesus Christ that you are now husband and wife, united in the sight of God and in the presence of this company. You may seal the marriage with a kiss.

## THE BLESSING

Now let us have a final prayer for your marriage: O God of Abraham and of Sarah, of Jacob and of Rachel, of Joseph and of Mary, of _____ and of _____, we commend to your safekeeping through their journey of life this couple who have taken the first step of their pilgrimage together. Guard them, we pray, from the disaffections and disappointments that would diminish their love. We do not ask that they be exempt from the trials and tribulations of life, as we all must face them, but grant that your Spirit may be upon them to lead them without harm. Help them to grow daily in their understanding of life and its values and to be flexible with each other and their families, that growth may be easy and exciting. Teach them to laugh about small problems and to pray about the greater ones. Enable them to negotiate their difficulties together, in order that the difficulties not divide them.

If by the grace of your creation they bring children into the world, give each of them a deep joy in parenthood, that the love and care within their home may issue in an even greater wholeness in their lives. Above all, O God, visit them with an abiding sense of your holy presence, that they may become witnesses of your divine grace in the manner of all their living and find pleasure not only in each other, but also in the world of all their goings and comings. Through Christ our Savior, who taught us to pray, saying:

**Our Father which art in heaven, Hallowed be thy name. Thy kingdom come, thy will be done in earth as it is in heaven. Give us this day our daily bread. And forgive us our debts as we forgive our debtors. And lead us not into temptation, but deliver us from evil: For thine is the kingdom, and the power, and the glory for ever. Amen.**

# IV.

---

# A SERVICE FOR
# A COUPLE WITH
# GROWN CHILDREN

7. PRAYER

8. Pronouncement : "By the power vested in me by the State of
Oregon ... husband & wife

9. Kiss : You may Kiss

10. Presentation : "Family & friends ... MR & MRS. James
Rudenko

## THE PROLOGUE

My friends, we are gathered here for a purpose both solemn and beautiful, both spiritual and of the earth. We are going to witness the marriage of _____ and _____, who have already promised themselves to each other in their hearts. It is a moment of enormous significance in their lives— perhaps of more significance than anything they have done in a long, long time or will ever do again; for from this moment their lives will grow differently—they will grow together. The way they see the world will be different. The way they relate to others will be different. And the way they know and experience each other will be different.

They are not beginners in life. Each has had a certain lifetime already, with experiences of pleasure and pain, of joy and agony, of discovery and growth. But their times for such experiences are not over. Their union, celebrated here today and forged by the days and years that lie ahead, will lead to new pleasures and pains, new times of discovery and growth. Therefore, this is a mystical time in their journeys, a time of great spiritual possibility. And thus it is a time to be remembered and celebrated before the altar of God, where the burning of candles symbolizes the presence of the Holy.

Because it is a time of spirit and celebration, we will pause to pray:

O God, who blesses all lives that are yielded to you in faith and sincerity, and without whom no life is ever blessed, we bow in your presence at the outset of this sacred experience. Give us all a sense of reverence for what we are about to do. Throughout human history, you have been especially close to persons whose lives were being brought into new relationships through marriage. Now, as _____ and _____ are joined before this altar, let us feel your closeness to them. Hallow the words we use and the air we breathe. Let the spirit and solemnity of this time never be lost to our memories, through him who loves us and sanctifies all our deeds, even Christ our Lord. **Amen.**

## THE BLESSING OF THE FAMILIES

What _____ and _____ do here affects the lives of others almost as profoundly as it affects their own lives. They have families whose relationships will be enlarged and with whom they now embark on a new adventure. We want to include the families and friends as well in our prayers and concern. So let us now pray for them:

O God, who is known in the encounter of person with person, family with family, and tribe with tribe, we magnify your name for being the One who binds all peoples together. In you, O Lord, shall all the nations of the world be blessed. Our days are as the grass which springs up today and tomorrow is cast into the oven, but your kingdom is forever. Teach us to find wisdom in our human limitations, and thereby to achieve more quickly the lessons of love and understanding.

We pray for these two families being united today, that the ties of relationship being occasioned by this wedding will soon be transcended by a sense of genuine community among them. Let your blessing rest especially upon the children, for whom this may seem strange and not a little difficult. May they receive comfort and understanding in their hearts and soon grow into a sense of love and security in their new relationships. Grant that this ceremony and what is accomplished here may lead us all into ever deeper experiences of your grace. Through Jesus Christ our Lord. **Amen.**

## THE PREPARATION

_____, as you stand before the altar of God in the presence of all these people, do you do so with a contrite heart, asking God's forgiveness for all your sins and seeking God's leadership in the new life upon which you will now embark?

*Bride:* **I do.**

_____, do you also, standing before the altar of God and in the presence of these people, come with a contrite heart, asking God's forgiveness for all your sins and seeking God's leadership in the new life upon which you will now embark?

*Groom:* **I do.**

## THE BLESSING OF THE RINGS

May I have the rings you intend to give each other? They are beautiful rings. Let us now have a prayer of blessing for them:

Lord, these rings are simple, like your plan for our lives and happiness. They are unbroken in their roundness, like the ages in your sight. They are things of value, like your word given to us by the prophets of old. Let them become living reminders, we pray, of the simple, unbroken, and valuable love that _____ and _____ have for each other.

Grant that nothing may complicate, break, or devalue that love. Teach them, whenever they look upon these symbols of affection, to remember this moment, this altar, this company of witnesses, this prayer, and your presence blessing their lives, surrounding them with goodness, and protecting them from evil. **Amen.**

## THE VOWS WITH THE EXCHANGE OF RINGS

_____, as you place your ring on _____'s finger and look into her eyes, please repeat after me the words of your sacred vow to her, taken before God and this company:

**I, _____, take you, _____, as my dear and lawful wife. I commit myself to you as your faithful husband, to honor you as a person, to love you as my companion, and to cherish you as a child of God. I intend the love I have for you now to be only the beginning of the love I will come to have as the years go by. I look forward to sharing my life with you, whatever the future holds, and I will comfort you, confide in you, and journey with you from this day forth, whatever the conditions of our lives or of the world around us. So help me, God.**

_____, as you look into _____'s eyes and place your ring on his finger, please repeat after me the words of your sacred vow to him:

I, _____, take you, _____, as my dear and lawful husband. I commit myself to you as your faithful wife, to honor you as a person, to love you as my companion, and to cherish you as a child of God. I intend the love I have for you now to be only the beginning of the love I will come to have as the years go by. I look forward to sharing my life with you, whatever the future holds, and I will comfort you, confide in you, and journey with you from this day forth, whatever the conditions of our lives or of the world around us. So help me, God.

## THE DECLARATION OF UNION

My friends, this is a joyous moment. By the authority vested in me by the church of Jesus Christ, I now name you husband and wife, joined of God in the presence of all these witnesses. May God enrich you forever through the union you have made and bless your families with the benefits of each new relationship. You may kiss and embrace each other in the joy of what we have done.

## THE PRAYER OF BLESSING

Now, having begun our celebration in the presence of the One whose holiness is commemorated by this altar, let us conclude by offering prayers of thanksgiving and supplication. Let us pray:

*A Service for a Couple with Grown Children*

We praise your loving mercy, O God, for the joy and excitement of this blessed occasion. It is you who has given us life and experience and you who has led us to this present moment. We acknowledge and bear you thanks for your everlasting care. Cast your mantle of grace and protection upon _____ and _____ as they begin this new phase of their journey through life. Safeguard them from perils both seen and unseen. Make them trustworthy to each other and to all whose lives are affected by their marriage. Teach them day by day to love more gently, care more deeply, and share more generously. Let the sun always rise upon their good will and let it never set without it. Abide in their home as the One who imparts value to their relationships and meaning to all their efforts. Shelter them from the tragedies so common to human life, or support them that they may stand when visited by adversity. And bring them at last, when life's journey is complete, to rest and repose in our Savior Jesus Christ, to whom be glory forever and ever, world without end, and in whose dear name we pray:

**Our Father which art in heaven, Hallowed be thy name. Thy kingdom come, thy will be done in earth as it is in heaven. Give us this day our daily bread. And forgive us our debts as we forgive our debtors. And lead us not into temptation, but deliver us from evil: For thine is the kingdom, and the power, and the glory for ever. Amen.**

*V.*

———

*A SERVICE FOR*

*AN OLDER COUPLE*

## THE PROLOGUE

God said, "It is not good that the man should be alone; I will make him a helpmeet for him" (Gen. 2:18 KJV). So from time immemorial man and woman have been together as helpers and companions. They are together because they would be lonely without each other; there is nothing slower than a rainy day in an empty house. They are together because they help and support each other; there is an old saying that "A man times a wife is equal to four." They are together because the life of each is fulfilled in the other: "Lovelier would this look," said the poet W. H. Auden, "if my love were with me." God has made us so that we see, hear, feel, and behave more completely in pairs than we do alone.

Thus it is good when two people who were alone,

as _____ and _____ were, come together.

Each has already had a lifetime, yet they still have a life ahead. The life that lies ahead is a gift, a time of grace to be spent in love and joy. The fever of youth wanes; the delight of age remains. Yet there is always something young about love—young and innocent and beautiful. It has made our friends young, innocent, and beautiful together.

Now we gather to celebrate in the eyes of the world what has already happened for them in the eyes of God, and to join them as husband and wife. If anyone objects to this, now is the time to speak. Otherwise, he or she should remain silent forever.

## THE EXCHANGE OF VOWS

_____ and _____, will you please join hands and look into each other's eyes as _____ says after me the words of his marriage vow:

**I, _____, take you, _____, for my lawful wedded wife. I promise to love you and care for you the rest of my life. As long as God gives me strength, I shall endeavor to make you happy and to share with you the blessedness of our hearth and home.**

Now, _____, will you please repeat the same vow after me:

I, _____, take you, _____, for my lawful wedded husband. I promise to love you and care for you the rest of my life. As long as God gives me strength, I shall endeavor to make you happy and to share with you the blessedness of our hearth and home.

Let us have a prayer to seal these vows:

O Lord, who in graciousness has given us the institution of marriage and in the Lord Jesus Christ has taught us the true meaning of love, that we should give ourselves for one another, we invoke your holy witness upon the words which _____ and _____ have spoken to each other in their wedding promises. Let your blessings rest upon them as long as they are true to them in your sight, and your displeasure if they ever become untrue. In the name of the Father, Son, and Holy Ghost. **Amen.**

## THE EXCHANGE OF RINGS

_____, will you now place on _____'s finger the ring you give her as a symbol of this marriage, and, continuing to look in her eyes, repeat after me the words of bestowal:

_____, I give you this ring as a sign of all my love. May it remain always to you and to others a symbol of my fidelity, and may God richly bless our union that is sealed herewith.

_____, will you repeat after me your words of acceptance:

_____, I accept your ring and will wear it as a symbol of my fidelity, and I say, also, may God richly bless our union that is sealed herewith.

_____, will you now place on _____'s finger the ring you give him as a symbol of this marriage, and, continuing to look in his eyes, repeat after me the words of bestowal:

_____, I give you this ring as a sign of all my love. May it remain always to you and to others a symbol of my fidelity, and may God richly bless our union that is sealed herewith.

_____, will you repeat after me your words of acceptance:

_____, I accept your ring and will wear it as a symbol of my fidelity, and I say, also, may God richly bless our union that is sealed herewith.

## THE PRONOUNCEMENT

_____ and _____, you have found each other in the mature years of your life on earth. You have discovered joy and delight in each other's presence. Now that you have pledged your love and faithfulness to each other, I take pleasure in pronouncing you husband and wife in the sight of both God and humanity. Will you grace the pronouncement with a kiss?

## THE BLESSING

Now let us pray for you as you begin together this new portion of your journey:

O God, who does not will that man or woman should be alone, but that together they should live and love and worship you, we join you and all your angels now in celebrating the marriage of _____ and _____. Let their days on earth be long and so filled with love and excitement that each one seems too brief. Give them the joy of simple moments spent together before an open fire, over the kitchen table, walking in a shopping mall, looking at old photographs, holding hands, and giving thanks for each other. Bless their children, that they may find happiness in the new relationships that have come to them, and in their parents' happiness. And teach us all, as we have strength, to live daily in your presence, humbling ourselves before mysteries we do not understand and giving thanks for bread and home and one another, for yours is the kingdom that makes our lives worthwhile, through Jesus Christ. **Amen.**

# VI.

---

## A SERVICE CELEBRATED BY TWO MINISTERS

## THE PROLOGUE

*First Minister:* The heart and soul of love is togetherness. The one thing love cannot abide is separation. This principle is set at the very center of life and faith. God created the world out of love. When the world denied that love—when sin caused separation in it—God did everything possible to bring us back into oneness with him. He even gave his only begotten Son to draw us back to himself.

*Second Minister:* One of the most beautiful stories Jesus ever told was the parable of a young man who withdrew from his father's household and came back again, producing great joy in his father's heart.

*First Minister:* When _____ and _____ present themselves to be joined in marriage, they are fulfilling the instinct for togetherness that God has implanted in all our hearts. They are helping to achieve the unity and harmony which are the goals of all creation and of God himself.

*Second Minister:* As we observe their love for each other, and their exchanging of vows, we shall all be refreshed in our sense of love and togetherness. The age-old ritual of joining a man and a woman will remind us deep within of the desire of God for the joyous unity of all created beings under his heavenly rule.

## THE BLESSING OF THE COUPLE

*First Minister:* Who blesses _____ as she and _____ come together in this act of love?

**Bride's Father: Her mother and I do.**

*Second Minister:* Who blesses _____ as he comes to be joined to _____?

**Groom's Father: His mother and I do.**

## THE QUESTIONING

*First Minister:* _____, is it your intention to marry _____ and have her as your wife, cherishing her and growing into oneness of heart and spirit with her for the rest of your life?

**Groom: It is.**

*First Minister:* _____, is it your intention to marry _____ and have him as your husband, cherishing him and growing into oneness of heart and spirit with him for the rest of your life?

*Bride:* **It is.**

## THE EXCHANGE OF VOWS

*First Minister:* Then let us proceed to the saying of your wedding promises. _____, will you please hold _____'s hand, and, looking into her eyes, repeat after me:

**I, _____, wed you, _____, in the spirit of the love that God has shown us both. I promise to care for you and to share my life with you as long as we both shall live. I pray that wherever our journey shall lead, through light or darkness, sickness or health, hard times or easy, we shall always be together, sealed in love, as Jesus Christ is my witness.**

_____, will you please hold _____'s hand, and, looking into his eyes, repeat the same words after me:

**I, _____, wed you _____, in the spirit of love that God has shown us both. I promise to care for you and to share my life with you as long as we**

**both shall live. I pray that wherever our journey shall lead, through light or darkness, sickness or health, hard times or easy, we shall always be together, sealed in love, as Jesus Christ is my witness.**

## THE BLESSING OF THE RINGS

*First Minister:* _____ and _____, will you now take the rings you intend to give each other and hold them as we have a prayer of blessing for them:

These rings, O Lord, are without end or beginning, like the eternity from which you see all finite moments. Let them remind _____ and _____ always to view life as you view it, and to care for each other as you care for them. As these rings are valuable tokens of esteem, costly in the world's economy, let them forever recall for _____ and _____ the worth with which they now regard each other, that they may never lose a sense of this esteem, and that the years may draw them ever more close to each other, in the name of the Father, Son, and Holy Spirit. **Amen.**

## THE EXCHANGE OF RINGS

*Second Minister:* _____ will you please place your ring on _____'s finger, and, continuing to hold her hand, repeat these words:

**I give you this ring as a sign of my love and pray that it may always remind us of this love, as a covenant of our care for each other from this day forward.**

_____, will you please place your ring on _____'s finger, and, continuing to hold his hand, repeat these words:

**I give you this ring as a sign of my love and pray that it may always remind us of this love, as a covenant of our care for each other from this day forward.**

The Lord's blessings be upon you both.

## THE DECLARATION OF MARRIAGE

*First Minister:* _____ and _____, because you have joined in this act of mutual profession of your care and desire to be together and have promised before this congregation to love and cherish each other from this day forth for the rest of your lives, I now pronounce you husband and wife, blessing your marriage in the name of the Father, the Son, and the Holy Ghost.

## LIGHTING THE UNITY CANDLE

*Second Minister:* As the flames of your two souls have burned alone during your childhood and adolescence, lighting your way to this precious moment, now they have begun to burn together and become one flame. To symbolize this new unity and togetherness, _____ and _____, you may now light the Unity Candle and extinguish the flames that have burned alone.

## THE PRAYER OF BLESSING

*First Minister:* Let us pray: Our Father, we thank you for the lives of these your children, united now in the bonds of marriage, and for the love that will find expression in such a union.

*Second Minister:* Grant to them, we pray, the presence and power of your Holy Spirit to be with them, to shelter them from adversity, and to strengthen them for the hard journey of life.

*First Minister:* Let them experience your support and encouragement in every undertaking, empowering them when they are weak and illumining their way when they are confused.

*Second Minister:* Give them faith to stand against the temptations of life and courage to admit their faults and shortcomings.

*First Minister:* Teach them to forgive each other's sins and to receive your mercy in their hearts.

*Second Minister:* Help them to celebrate the beauty of their daily life together, relishing the moments of insight, the individual differences that perplex and enrich them, and the opportunity they have to worship you in acts of kindness to each other.

*First Minister:* If they become parents, lead them quickly to the deeper delights of family love.

*Second Minister:* Enable them to share love as it has been shared with them.

*First Minister:* Let their families be wise to support them when they need support and stand aside when they should find their way alone.

*Second Minister:* Help them to feel our genuine care for them and to know they walk always in our love.

*First Minister:* Now let your benediction be upon them in this hour and all the times to come, leading them in paths of righteousness for your name's sake.

*Second Minister:* And hear us all as we pray together the prayer our Lord has given us saying:

**Our Father which art in heaven, Hallowed be thy name. Thy kingdom come, thy will be done in earth as it is in heaven. Give us this day our daily bread. And forgive us our debts as we forgive our debtors. And lead us not into temptation, but deliver us from evil: For thine is the kingdom, and the power, and the glory for ever.** Amen.

## THE SACRAMENT OF COMMUNION

*First Minister:* Because you have wished it, _____ and _____, your first meal together as husband and wife will be a holy meal, the sacrament of our Lord's Table. There is no more fitting way to set upon your journey than this, which is to insure your strength of spirit and your sense of commitment to God, who will keep you always as long as your faith is stayed on him.

*Second Minister:* Let us remember how the Lord Jesus, on the night when he was betrayed, took bread, and having blessed it, he gave it to the disciples and said, "Take, eat; this is my body, which is broken for you. This do in remembrance of me." And in the same manner he took the cup, after supper, and when he had blessed it he gave it to them and said, "This cup is the new covenant in my blood. All of you drink of this." As often as we eat this bread and drink this cup, we commemorate the Lord's death until he returns.

*First Minister:* We thank you, O most merciful and everlasting Father, for this holy bread and cup, which you have given as reminders of the suffering and death of your Son Jesus, who is present with us now in the spirit of his resurrection. Cleanse us of all guilt and unworthiness and give us penitent, receptive hearts, that we may receive these gifts in joy and gratitude and become your humble servants this night and evermore. Through him whose name is beyond all names of men and of angels, even Christ our Lord.

(Distribution to _____ and _____.)

## BENEDICTION

*Second Minister:* Now, may God, whose everlasting Spirit has brought us into divine union with his love and purpose for our lives, and who continues to go before us in the way, bless and keep you from this time forth, shielding you from every danger, both without and within; may he show you mercy in all your failings, and make you patient with one another; and may he bring you at last unto eternal life, to dwell with him forever and ever, world without end and joy beyond compare; in the name of the Father, and of the Son, and of the Holy Ghost. **Amen.**

# VII.

———

# A SERVICE WITH
# A GUEST MINISTER
# ASSISTING

## THE PROLOGUE

My friends, we are gathered here today for one of the happiest occasions in all human life, to celebrate before God the marriage of a man and a woman who love each other. Those of us who are members of (host church) welcome our friends from other churches, and especially (guest minister) of (guest minister's church), who joins me as an officient in the ceremony. We are all part of the household of God, and our celebration is more complete because you are here.

(Guest minister) will now read from the Holy Scriptures:

> Genesis 2:18, 21-24
> Ruth 1:16-17
> I Corinthians 13:4-8*a*

The Bible is filled with references to the holy estate of marriage. Paul even speaks of the church as the bride of Christ, suggesting the reverence in which weddings are held by the scriptures. It is God's will that all the people of the world be one, and marriage helps to fulfill that will. When _____ and _____ are united in marriage, the world will be closer to God's vision for it. Not only will they be joined together, but also their families will be related in important new ways. Therefore, we follow the tradition in weddings of asking the blessings of the parents upon their children's marriage.

## THE BLESSING

Who gives a blessing upon _____ as she marries _____?

(Guest Minister) will lead us in a prayer for the families of _____ and _____ as they are united by this ceremony.

*Guest Minister:* Let us pray:

O God, who has made of one blood all the people of the world and who calls us to a spirit of unity and love with one another, we lift up before you these two families about to be related by marriage. Give them your grace to enjoy one another and to appreciate the gifts that each brings to the other. Teach them to be wise parents, gladly releasing their children into a new household. Help them to be supportive of the children and of one another, that the new relationships may flourish and grow and that their own lives may be blessed by the joy and good will of all. And let them come at last, with all of us, to the consummation of life in your kingdom, knowing that their way has been true and good, and enriched by what we are doing here today. In the name of the Father, Son, and Holy Ghost. **Amen.**

## *THE EXCHANGE OF RINGS AND VOWS*

Now, _____ and _____, we symbolize the importance of what we are about to do by moving into the chancel area of the church. The taking of marriage vows before God is a very serious matter. You will be pledging your faithfulness not only to each other but also to God. Those who remember the sacredness of their vows are blessed by them all their lives; those who forget will find them a curse. Are you willing, as you stand before God, your families, and friends, to proceed to the exchange of vows?

*Bride and Groom:* **We are.**

Then let us proceed.

First, will you please take the rings you will give each other and hold them as we offer a prayer for their meaning.

Let us pray:

Father of all blessedness, who bestows a ring and a robe upon every wayward child returning to your household, we present to you now these lovely rings that _____ and _____ will wear for the rest of their lives. Make them tokens of faithfulness from this day forward. Let their shining beauty remind _____ and _____ always of this shining moment in their lives. And grant that wearing them may always be an honor and a pleasure to them, recalling the deep love that has brought them together. Through our Lord Jesus Christ. **Amen.**

_____, will you please put your ring on _____'s finger and continue to hold her hand, looking into her eyes as you repeat your vow after me:

**I, _____, receive you, _____, as the wife I will cherish the rest of my life. I promise to love you, care for you, and grow with you through the years. Everything I have is yours. I will cleave to you in sickness and in health, in good times and bad, as long as we both shall live. So help me, God.**

_____, will you please put your ring on _____'s finger, and looking into his eyes, continue to hold his hand as you repeat your vow after me:

I, _____, receive you, _____, as the husband I will cherish the rest of my life. I promise to love you, care for you, and grow with you through the years. Everything I have is yours. I will cleave to you in sickness and in health, in good times and bad, as long as we both shall live. So help me, God.

## THE PRONOUNCEMENT

_____ and _____, because you have confessed your great love for each other, and because you have made your vows of marriage before God and in the company of all these people, I now declare that you are husband and wife. May God seal in eternity the contract you have made here, and enable you to live by it all of your lives, in the name of the Father, Son, and Holy Ghost. You may, if you wish, complete the ceremony with an embrace and a kiss.

## THE PRAYER

Let us all pray:

God of power and holiness, who gives us the kingdom and then bids us to live in such a way as to claim it, we celebrate in your presence the union of _____ and _____. Dwell in them, we pray, to make them truly one. Enable them to break down one by one the walls that may exist between them, discovering the importance of honesty and the beauty of intimacy. Grant to them a quality of love that will overcome all brokenness and misunderstanding in their lives. Let each of them live so completely in the awareness of your redeeming presence that they shall always have an instinct for wholeness and communion with each other.

If their marriage is enriched by the coming of children, teach them to be fond and adoring parents, slow to anger and resentment, and quick to caring and forgiveness. Guide them in the establishment of life's patterns together, that these may be wholesome and nourishing to their continued joy and well-being.

Make them generous in their response to the community around them, thoughtful in their dealings with parents and other relations, and wise in their choice of friendships. Give them loyalty to the church, discretion in the ordering of their finances, and strength of character for the fulfillment of all their obligations.

Above all, implant faith in their hearts, that they may live always in the expectancy of your grace and know that all human life, including that of a married couple, reaches its highest moment when it says yes to you. To that end, let this entire congregation worship you and say yes through our Lord Jesus Christ, who taught us to pray devoutly, saying:

**Our Father which art in heaven, Hallowed be thy name. Thy kingdom come, thy will be done in**

**earth as it is in heaven. Give us this day our daily bread. And forgive us our debts as we forgive our debtors. And lead us not into temptation, but deliver us from evil: For thine is the kingdom, and the power, and the glory for ever.** Amen.

*Guest Minister:* Now may grace, mercy, and peace be upon this couple and upon every one of us, keeping us always in perfect union with the Father who loves us, the Son who died for us, and the Holy Spirit who lives in us, today and evermore. **Amen.**

# VIII.

—

# A SERVICE AT
# CHRISTMAS

## THE PROLOGUE

In the Christmas season, we celebrate the incarnation of God in human flesh. "The Word became flesh and dwelt among us." We remember from the imagery of animals around a manger and shepherds coming from their fields what it means for God to be housed among us.

What more wonderful time could there be for a wedding, and remembering God's concern for human relationships and marriage? Carols renew our joy in the created world, and the burning of candles reminds us of God's presence in the home. The bells of Christmas become the bells of weddings, tolling out the news of God becoming man and of man and woman becoming husband and wife.

You are all welcome here as _____ and _____ open their hearts and say their marriage vows to each other. It is a time of beauty and festivity, of mystery and grace. It is their time, and our time, and God's time.

Because it is God's time, and God is most important, let us pray:

We lift our hearts to you, O God, for the wonder and marvel of this Advent time, and for the many reminders it brings of the birth of our Savior. We hold before you _____ and _____, who are here to be joined in marriage, and their families, who will be enlarged and changed by this union. May the angels that sang over Bethlehem now sing of this wedding, rejoicing at this new bond in which your Spirit may become incarnate. We bow before you as the shepherds bowed in the lowly stable and follow a star of love that the wise men followed. Give heavenly sanction to what we do, that the intertwining of _____'s and _____'s lives may bring earthly glory to your name. **Amen.**

_____, do you, standing in this holy place and upheld by the affection of these friends and loved ones, wish publicly to declare your love and esteem for _____, to be joined to her in the sacred bonds of marriage for the rest of your life, and to have that marriage blessed by the God who came among us in Jesus Christ?

***Groom:*** **I do.**

_____, do you, standing in this holy place and upheld by the affection of these friends and loved ones, wish publicly to declare your love and esteem for _____, to be joined to him in the sacred bonds of marriage for the rest of your life, and to have that marriage blessed by the God who came among us in Jesus Christ?

***Bride:*** **I do.**

Mary and Joseph, the parents, hold a central place in the story of Jesus' birth. Parents are likewise very important here, for they have invested much of themselves in the rearing of _____ and _____. Therefore, we follow the wedding custom of asking who gives _____ to be married to _____, and in so doing honor not only _____'s father but also her mother and _____'s father and mother. Who gives _____ to be married to _____?

***Bride's father:*** **Her mother and I do.**

May God be in what we are about to do here, as God was in the events surrounding the birth of Jesus, and as he continued to be in the life and ministry of our Lord.

## THE EXCHANGE OF VOWS

_____, will you please repeat after me the words of your wedding vow to _____.

I, _____, take you, _____, to be my dearest life's companion, and engage to be your faithful husband. I promise to make every effort toward the success of our marriage, and toward understanding your needs and feelings. I will stand by you in all the seasons of our life, in times of darkness as well as light. Your sorrows will be my sorrows, and your pleasures will be mine as well. I love you now, and I hope to love you more tomorrow and in all the tomorrows after that. As the Child of Bethlehem grew to manhood, may God enable our caring for each other to grow to full maturity in his perfect grace and wisdom.

_____, will you please repeat after me the words of your wedding vow to _____.

I, _____, take you, _____, to be my dearest life's companion, and engage to be your faithful wife. I promise to make every effort toward the success of our marriage, and toward understanding your needs and feelings. I will stand by you in all the seasons of our life, in times of darkness as well as light. Your sorrows will be my sorrows, and your pleasures will be mine as well. I love you now, and I hope to love you more tomorrow and in all the tomorrows after that. As the Child of Bethlehem grew to manhood, may God enable our caring for each other to grow to full maturity in his perfect grace and wisdom.

## THE EXCHANGE OF RINGS

The only rings in the Christmas legends are the five golden rings of the popular song. We remember, however, that the father in Jesus' story of the prodigal son bestowed upon his son a ring as a symbol of family membership, and it is entirely possible that Jesus' earthly father Joseph once gave him such a ring. The rings that _____ and _____ will now exchange are likewise symbols of family membership, of a very special kind. _____ and _____, will you please hold your rings as we bless them in God's name:

These golden rings, O God, are the signs of _____'s and _____'s love for each other. They are gifts of the highest order, symbolizing fidelity, eternity, and relationship. Bless them now with the power always to remind _____ and _____ of their vows to each other and of this special moment when they exchanged them. Let peace and love attend this couple as long as they wear these rings. Through Jesus Christ our Lord. **Amen.**

_____, will you please place your ring on _____'s finger and repeat these words after me:

**With this ring I give you my heart and say proudly to the world, "This is my wife, whom I cherish above all others now and ever more."**

_____, will you please place your ring on _____'s finger and repeat these words after me:

**With this ring I give you my heart and say proudly to the world, "This is my husband, whom I cherish above all others now and ever more."**

## THE PRONOUNCEMENT

_____ and _____, because you have consented to belong to each other for the rest of your lives and have given your vows before this company of friends and relatives and have sealed your words by the giving and receiving of rings, I am happy to pronounce you husband and wife and to declare you joined forever in the sight of God. In the spirit of the season, you may give each other a kiss.

## THE BLESSING

Now let us pray:
O God, who descended to earth so long ago in the little town of Bethlehem, descend to us now, we

pray, to bless this marriage. Let the Spirit of Christ be upon _____ and _____, that each may live humbly toward the other, while exploring the power of love to seal and transform their relationship. Grant peace and prosperity to their household and teach them to be generous with all who now live or come to live in their midst. Make them wise parents who will impart both love and strength to their children. Bestow upon them forgiveness for all their sins and enable them to live from day to day with a sense of newness. Heal whatever wounds or scars they carry into their relationship, and let them in turn deal gently with all others. Let the giving of gifts, so natural at Christmas time, be natural for them at all other times as well, that they may be thoughtful and caring, encouraging each other in gracious ways. Make them strong in times of trouble, flexible in times of conflict, and responsive in times of learning. Now let the bells of heaven sound with joy at the birth of the Savior and at the beginning of this marriage, that we may all celebrate with _____ and _____ the grace that has come into their lives. Through Jesus Christ our Lord. **Amen.**

# IX.

---

## A SERVICE AT
## EASTER

## THE PROLOGUE

Easter is the most special day of the Christian calendar. It is a time of springing grass and flowering trees, of jonquils and tulips and Easter lilies, of sweet-smelling earth and blue skies and waving willow branches. It is the time when all nature seems to echo the truth of Christ's resurrection from the dead and remind us that God's last word, when all other words have been spoken, is not *die* but *live!*

By the same token, a wedding is the most special day on any couple's calendar—the day when they join hands, say their vows, and know that somehow, in the mystery of God, they have been united in the sight of heaven and all their friends. It is a day of new beginnings, of growth and experience, and an open road to be taken, not alone, but together.

For the two days to fall together, a wedding on Easter, is beautiful and appropriate for Christians being united, because it says that their special day, in their own minds and hearts, yields in importance to the day of Christ's resurrection and derives its inner strength and meaning from the fact that he is alive forevermore. The wedding thus becomes a witness to faith, and the faith may be counted on as an eternal source of power and reverence in their marriage. The risen Christ stands, as it were, at the center of their lives together, blessing and guaranteeing the contract they make with each other.

Let us offer a prayer of thanksgiving for this doubly special occasion:

O God, whose nature is known in the love that was crucified at Calvary and the life that was manifested by an empty tomb, we lift our voices in praise and thanksgiving for Easter, which is the most glorious reminder of that life, and for the wedding of _____ and _____, which is to be effected now, while the sound of hallelujahs still rings in our ears and hearts. Grant that the power which returned our Lord Jesus from the grave may seal and protect what we do here and lend added joy and meaning to the taking of vows in his name. **Amen.**

## THE ACKNOWLEDGEMENT

_____, do you acknowledge your deep affection for _____ and your desire for her to be your wife, and do you intend, renouncing all others, to cling to her henceforth as the dearest person in your life, seeking her happiness as well as your own and preferring her welfare even to yours?

*Groom:* **I do.**

_____, do you likewise acknowledge your deep affection for _____ and your desire for him to be your husband, and do you intend, renouncing all others, to cling to him henceforth as the dearest person in your life, seeking his happiness as well as your own and preferring his welfare even to yours?

*Bride:* **I do.**

## THE EXCHANGE OF VOWS

_____, will you please hold _____'s hand, and, looking into her eyes, repeat the words of your wedding vow:

**I, _____, take you, _____, as my lawful, wedded wife, to love and to cherish, to support and to honor the rest of our lives together. I promise to work at our marriage, that we may always be open and generous with each other about the things that matter most. And I invoke the presence of the risen Christ to watch over us and ours and to bring us into his eternal kingdom to dwell with him forever.**

_____, will you please hold _____'s hand, and, looking into his eyes, repeat the words of your wedding vow:

I, _____, take you, _____, as my lawful, **wedded husband, to love and to cherish, to support and to honor the rest of our lives together. I promise to work at our marriage, that we may always be open and generous with each other about the things that matter most. And I invoke the presence of the risen Christ to watch over us and ours and to bring us into his eternal kingdom to dwell with him forever.**

## THE EXCHANGE OF RINGS

Do you have rings to exchange? Let us have a prayer for them:

O God, these beautiful rings are circular and seamless, like the fullness of eternity in your love. Endow them with the deep significance of this moment, we pray, that they may always remind _____ and _____ of the vows they have made to each other and guard their care for each other through the years. In the name of the Father, Son, and Holy Ghost. **Amen.**

_____, will you please slip your ring onto _____'s finger and repeat these words as you continue to hold her hand:

_____, I give you this ring as token of my love and pledge to remember this moment. May it forever recall the holiness of what we have done here and keep us faithful to each other throughout life's journey.

_____, will you please slip your ring onto _____'s finger and repeat these words as you continue to hold his hand:

_____, I give you this ring as token of my love and pledge to remember this moment. May it forever recall the holiness of what we have done here and keep us faithful to each other throughout life's journey.

## THE PRONOUNCEMENT

_____ and _____, because you have declared your love for each other and your desire to live together as husband and wife, and because you have made vows of affection and faithfulness that will remain with you all your lives, I take great pleasure this Easter day in pronouncing you husband and wife, deserving of each other and blessed of God. Would you like to seal the pronouncement with a kiss?

## THE BLESSING

O God of a bloodstained cross and an empty tomb, who has known the hard realities of human life and yet transcends it in power and holiness, we commit to you for your love and watchcare _____ and _____, that you may be their unseen companion in the pilgrimage before them. Comfort them in the hours of their need, when difficulties arise and tensions mount, that they may draw upon the strength beyond their own and find in the beauty of their marriage an even greater channel for the receiving of your grace. Give them wisdom in times of joy to see in you the source of all our pleasure, and thus to draw ever closer to you and to each other in the heavenly way. Grant peace and happiness to each of their children, that they may celebrate with the parents a sense of the higher presence in their home, and find in one another ministering spirits of love and kindness. And now, in the company of all these friends and family members, we praise you once more for the raising of our Savior and pray together the prayer he has taught us to pray, saying:

**Our Father which art in heaven, Hallowed be thy name. Thy kingdom come, thy will be done in earth as it is in heaven. Give us this day our daily bread. And forgive us our debts as we forgive our debtors. And lead us not into temptation, but deliver us from evil: For thine is the kingdom, and the power, and the glory for ever. Amen.**

And now may the God of Easter time, who has brought again from the dead our Lord Jesus Christ, bring the gospel of the resurrection to its full fruition in our lives, that we may all live in joy and peace with one another, confirming one another in love and blessedness, now and forever. In the name of the Father, Son, and Holy Ghost. **Amen.**